RHEUMATOID ARTHRITIS COOKBOOK

MAIN COURSE – 80+ Effective recipes designed to treat inflammation and reduce pain with specific nutritional information (Proved recipes to treat joint pain)

TABLE OF CONTENTS

- LUNCH 7
- RISOTO WITH CRIMINI MUSHROOMS 7
- ASPARAGUS WITH QUINCE JAM 9
- FENEL CUCUMBER SALAD 10
- SALMON SALAD 11
- APPLE SOUP 12
- CARROT SALAD WITH GINGER 13
- CARROT SOUP 14
- POTATO SOUP 15
- BARLEY SOUP 16
- NETTLE SOUP 17
- LENTIL SOUP 19
- OMELET WITH RED ONIONS 20
- BROCCOLI SALAD WITH APPLES 22
- BEET AND CARROT SOUP 23
- SMOKED SALMON SALAD 24
- BARLEY SOUP WITH CARROTS 25
- PASTA WITH NETTLE PESTO 26
- ONION SOUP 27
- ASPARAGUS WITH QUINOA NOODLES 28
- CUCUMER SALAD 30
- BARLEY SOUP WITH CARROTS 31
- ONION SOUP 33
- CARROT SOUP 34
- SWEET POTATO SOUP 36

BROCCOLI SOUP	37
LENTIL SOUP	39
NETTLE & SHALLOT SOUP	41
ASPAGARUS WITH QUINCE JAM	43
RISOTTO WITH MUSHROOMS	44
BROCCOLI SALAD	46
SMOKED SALMON SALAD	47
CUCUMBER SALAD	48
SALMON SALAD	49
CARROT FENNEL SALAD	50
CARROT SALAD WITH GINGER	51
THAI PUMPKIN SOUP	52
POTATOES WITH POACHED EGGS	53
TUNA SALAD	55
TURKEY CHILI	56
TILAPIA WITH ROSEMARY TOPPING	58
DINNER	60
ROASTED EGGPLANT DIE	60
SPINACH SPREAD	62
LENTIL HUMMUS	64
CUMIN SCENTED BEAN DIP	65
CHIPOTLE BEAN SOUP	66
BEAN AND CORN TACOS	67
BLACK BEAN SALAD WITH QUINOA	68
CREAMY SCRAMBLED EGGS	69
CHICKEN CURRY WITH BROWN RICE	70

MEXICAN BROWN RICE	70
LEMON ROSEMARY CHICKEN	72
PAN CON TOMATE	74
MARINATED CHEESE	75
MARINATED LAMB SKEWERS	76
TUNA SANDWICH WITH EGG AND OLIVES	78
SHRIMP SKEWERS WITH GARLIC	79
SEEDED RICE	80
SESAME TOFU	81
HUEVOS RANCHEROS	83
SWISS, HAM AND AVOCADO SCRAMBLE	84
DESSERT	85
RICE PUDDING	85
BLUEBERRY SOUP	86
PINEAPLLE SMOOTHIE	87
APPLE AND RASPBERRY CRUMBLE	88
RASPBERRY BANANA SMOOTHIE	89
APPLE SLICES WITH CINNAMON	90
QUINOA CREPES	91
BANANA MUFFINS	92
ANTIOXIDANT MUFFINS	93
CANTALOUPE SMOOTHIE	95
CARROT MUFFINS	96
TURMERIC SMOOTHIE	97
PINEAPPLE SMOOTHIE	98
BLUEBERRY KALE SMOOTHIE	99

VANILLA PROTEIN SMOOTHIE	100
BROCCOLI SMOOTHIE	101
TROPICAL SMOOTHIE	102
GREEN SMOOTHIE	103
BERRY SMOOTHIE	104
CHERRY PIE SMOOTHIE	105

Copyright 2018 by Noah Jerris - All rights reserved.

This document is geared towards providing exact and reliable information in regards to the topic and issue covered. The publication is sold with the idea that the publisher is not required to render accounting, officially permitted, or otherwise, qualified services. If advice is necessary, legal or professional, a practiced individual in the profession should be ordered.

- From a Declaration of Principles which was accepted and approved equally by a Committee of the American Bar Association and a Committee of Publishers and Associations.

In no way is it legal to reproduce, duplicate, or transmit any part of this document in either electronic means or in printed format. Recording of this publication is strictly prohibited and any storage of this document is not allowed unless with written permission from the publisher. All rights reserved.

The information provided herein is stated to be truthful and consistent, in that any liability, in terms of inattention or otherwise, by any usage or abuse of any policies, processes, or directions contained within is the solitary and utter responsibility of the recipient reader. Under no circumstances will any legal responsibility or blame be held against the publisher for any reparation, damages, or monetary loss due to the information herein, either directly or indirectly.

Respective authors own all copyrights not held by the publisher.

The information herein is offered for informational purposes solely, and is universal as so. The presentation of the information is without contract or any type of guarantee assurance.

The trademarks that are used are without any consent, and the publication of the trademark is without permission or backing by the trademark owner. All trademarks and brands within this book are for clarifying purposes only and are the owned by the owners themselves, not affiliated with this document.

Introduction

Rheumatoid arthritis recipes for autoimmune problems but also for family enjoyment. You will love them for sure for how easy it is to prepare them.

LUNCH

RISOTO WITH CRIMINI MUSHROOMS

Serves: **4**

Prep Time: **10** Minutes

Cook Time: **20** Minutes

Total Time: **30** Minutes

INGREDIENTS

- ½ lbs. crimini mushrooms
- 3 tablespoons olive oil
- ½ cups whine wine
- 1 onion
- 1 cup brown rice
- 3 cup chicken broth
- 2 tablespoons parsley
- 1 garlic clove
- ½ cup parmesan cheese
- 1 tsp salt
- ¼ lb. zucchini

DIRECTIONS

1. Heat 1 tablespoon olive oil in a saucepan
2. Add zucchini, mushrooms and season with salt and cook until soft
3. In a sauce pan add olive oil and onion and cook for 4-5 minutes
4. Add rice and cook for 3-4 minutes and add wine
5. Add broth and, zucchini, parsley, mushrooms and stir in olive oil
6. Add parmesan, salt and serve

ASPARAGUS WITH QUINCE JAM

Serves: **4**

Prep Time: **10** Minutes

Cook Time: **10** Minutes

Total Time: **20** Minutes

INGREDIENTS

- 1-lb asparagus spears
- 2 tablespoons walnuts
- 1 tsp salt
- 1 tsp fresh ginger
- 1 tsp quince jam
- 1 tsp olive oil

DIRECTIONS

1. Prepare a steamer with boiling water
2. Add asparagus and cook for 4-5 minutes and transfer asparagus to a plate
3. In a bowl whisk quince jam, lemon juice, ginger, salt and pepper
4. Pour over asparagus and serve

FENEL CUCUMBER SALAD

Serves: **4**

Prep Time: **10** Minutes

Cook Time: **10** Minutes

Total Time: **20** Minutes

INGREDIENTS

- 5 carrots
- 1 fennel bulb
- 1 cucumber
- ¼ cup fresh mint
- 3 tablespoons squeezed lemon
- 1 tablespoons canola oil

DIRECTIONS

1. In a bowl mix cucumber, mint, carrots and fennel
2. Pour lemon juice and oil in a jar and shake
3. Pour dressing over salad and serve

SALMON SALAD

Serves: 2
Prep Time: **10** Minutes
Cook Time: **40** Minutes
Total Time: **50** Minutes

INGREDIENTS

- 2 fillets salmon
- 1 tablespoon balsamic vinegar
- 1 tablespoon olive oil
- ½ tsp pepper
- 1 cup cucumber
- 1 onion
- 1 tablespoon capers
- 1 tablespoon fresh dill

DIRECTIONS

1. Bake the salmon in the oven for 20-25 minutes
2. Remove skin and bones and break into small chunks
3. Add capers, cucumber and onion
4. Add olive oil, vinegar and dill in a bowl
5. Add salt and refrigerate for 25-30 minute

APPLE SOUP

Serves: **4**

Prep Time: **10** Minutes

Cook Time: **30** Minutes

Total Time: **40** Minutes

INGREDIENTS

- 1 tablespoon canola oil
- 1 onion
- 1 small leek
- ½ tablespoons rosemary
- ½ tablespoons fresh thyme
- 2 apples
- 5 cups vegetable broth

DIRECTIONS

1. In a saucepan heat olive oil over medium heat
2. Add onions and sauté until brown
3. Pour the broth to the boil over medium heat
4. Add apples, reduce heat and simmer for 10 minutes
5. Serve when ready

CARROT SALAD WITH GINGER

Serves: 2
Prep Time: 10 Minutes
Cook Time: 20 Minutes
Total Time: 30 Minutes

INGREDIENTS

- ¼ cup raw beets
- 1 tablespoon apple juice
- 1 tablespoon olive oil
- ¼ ginger
- ¼ tsp salt
- ½ cup carrots

DIRECTIONS

1. Mix carrots and beets in a bowl
2. Mix ginger, salt, juice and olive in another bowl and mix over salad mixture

CARROT SOUP

Serves: **4**

Prep Time: **10** Minutes

Cook Time: **30** Minutes

Total Time: **40** Minutes

INGREDIENTS

- 2 beets
- 1 onion
- 1 tablespoon ginger
- 1 garlic clove
- 5 cups vegetable stock
- 1 tablespoon olive oil

DIRECTIONS

1. In a saucepan heat oil over medium heat
2. Sauce onion until golden brown
3. Add ginger, garlic and cook for 2-3 minutes
4. Add carrots, stock and beets
5. Reduce heat and simmer until tender for 20-25 minutes
6. Remove and serve garnished with cilantro leaves

POTATO SOUP

Serves: **4**

Prep Time: **10** Minutes

Cook Time: **30** Minutes

Total Time: **40** Minutes

INGREDIENTS

- 1 tablespoon canola oil
- 1-lbs. sweet potatoes
- ½ inch fresh ginger
- 2 cups low-sodium vegetable broth
- parsley
- 1 onion
- 1 clove garlic
- 1 tsp curry powder

DIRECTIONS

1. In a saucepan heat oil over medium heat
2. Add garlic, curry powder and cook for 1-2 minutes
3. Add onion, potatoes, broth and let it boil for 20 minutes

4. Puree soup in blender and blend until smooth
5. Top with parsley

BARLEY SOUP

Serves: 2

Prep Time: **10** Minutes

Cook Time: **20** Minutes

Total Time: **30** Minutes

INGREDIENTS

- ½ cup yellow onion
- ¼ dried marjoram
- 1 tsp thyme
- 1 cup
- 1 carrot
- 1 rig organic celery
- 1 tablespoon olive oil
- 3 cup broccoli

DIRECTIONS

1. In a pot cook onion over medium heat for 4-5 minutes

2. Add vegetable broth and bring to boil
3. Simmer and add celery and carrots
4. Cover and let simmer
5. Add barley, tomatoes, garlic and marjoram
6. Season with salt and serve

NETTLE SOUP

Serves: 2

Prep Time: 10 Minutes

Cook Time: 20 Minutes

Total Time: 30 Minutes

INGREDIENTS

- 5 oz. nettle tips
- 4 oz. spinach
- 1 cup organic milk
- 2 tablespoons flour
- white pepper
- nutmeg
- 2 tablespoons olive oil
- 1 shallot

- 1 cup water

DIRECTIONS

1. In a saucepan heat olive oil and add onion over medium heat
2. Add nettle, spinach, water and bring to boil, cook until tender
3. Whisk cold milk and flour in a bowl
4. Pour into saucepan and whisk to blend
5. Bring to boil and simmer for a few minutes, season with salt, pepper and nutmeg

LENTIL SOUP

Serves: 2

Prep Time: 10 Minutes

Cook Time: 30 Minutes

Total Time: 40 Minutes

INGREDIENTS

- 2 tablespoons olive oil
- 1 cup red lentils
- 28 oz. canned tomatoes
- 5 cup vegetable stock
- 1 tsp salt
- 1 tsp black pepper
- Greek yoghurt
- 1 onion
- 1 carrot
- 1 clove garlic
- 1 tsp ginger
- 1 tsp cumin
- 1 tsp coriander seeds

DIRECTIONS

1. Crush and mint garlic
2. In a saucepan add onion and cook for 4-5 minutes
3. Add lentils, carrots, coriander, canned tomatoes, cumin, salt and bring to boil
4. Cover and let simmer for 20-25 minutes
5. Add garlic and simmer for 4-5 minutes
6. Spoon soup into bowl and top with yoghurt

OMELET WITH RED ONIONS

Serves: **4**

Prep Time: **10** Minutes

Cook Time: **10** Minutes

Total Time: **20** Minutes

INGREDIENTS

- 3 eggs
- 1 tablespoon olive oil
- 1 tablespoon water
- ½ tsp salt
- 1 onion
- 2 tsp capers

DIRECTIONS

1. Grease a frying pan with olive oil and add onion
2. In a bowl mix salt, water and eggs
3. Add capers to mixture and pour over onions
4. Cook until ready and remove from pan

BROCCOLI SALAD WITH APPLES

Serves: 2
Prep Time: 10 Minutes
Cook Time: 20 Minutes
Total Time: 30 Minutes

INGREDIENTS

- 3 cup broccoli
- ½ cup cranberries
- ½ cup sunflower seeds
- 2 apples
- ½ cup onion
- 1 cup yoghurt
- 1 tablespoon mustard
- ½ cup honey

DIRECTIONS

1. Mix seeds, apples, broccoli, cranberries and onion in a bowl
2. In a blender add honey, yoghurt and honey
3. Add dressing to the salad and toss

BEET AND CARROT SOUP

Serves: **2**

Prep Time: **10** Minutes

Cook Time: **30** Minutes

Total Time: **40** Minutes

INGREDIENTS

- 2 beets
- 1 cup onion
- 1 lb. ginger
- 1 garlic clove
- 5 cups vegetable stock
- 1 tablespoon olive oil

DIRECTIONS

1. In a saucepan heat oil over medium heat
2. Sauté onion and add ginger and garlic and cook for 3-4 minutes
3. Add beets, stock and carrots, reduce heat and simmer for 20-25 minutes
4. In a food processor puree soup and taste
5. Serve hot and garnish with cilantro leaves

SMOKED SALMON SALAD

Serves: **4**

Prep Time: **10** Minutes

Cook Time: **30** Minutes

Total Time: **40** Minutes

INGREDIENTS

- 1 romaine lettuce
- ½ lemon
- 1tsp ginger root
- 1 tablespoon canola oil
- 4 ounces smoked salmon
- 1 tomatoes
- 3 radishes
- 1 carrot
- ¼ cucumber

DIRECTIONS

1. On a place add romaine lettuce with tomatoes, radishes, salmon, cucumber and carrots
2. In a jar add canola oil, ginger and lemon juice
3. Pour over salad

BARLEY SOUP WITH CARROTS

Serves: 2

Prep Time: 10 Minutes

Cook Time: 50 Minutes

Total Time: 60 Minutes

INGREDIENTS

- 1/3 cup water
- 1/3 cup parsley
- ½ tsp pepper
- 1/3 tsp black pepper
- 1/3 cup barley
- 1 tablespoon olive oil
- ½ cup onion
- 1 cup carrots
- 1 cup vegetable stock
- 1 cup plain yogurt

DIRECTIONS

1. In a pot bring water to boil
2. Add barley and simmer 20-25 minutes over low heat

3. In a pot cook onion and olive oil for 4-5 minutes, add carrots and boil for 20-25 minutes
4. Add barley and let simmer, remove from heat
5. Stir in yoghurt and serve

PASTA WITH NETTLE PESTO

Serves: 3
Prep Time: 10 Minutes
Cook Time: 20 Minutes
Total Time: 30 Minutes

INGREDIENTS

- 1 cup nettle leaves
- ½ cup parmesan cheese
- ½ cup olive oil
- 10 oz. pasta
- 3 garlic cloves
- ½ cup walnuts

DIRECTIONS

1. In a food processor add garlic, walnuts and leaves

2. Blend until smooth and olive oil and stir in parmesan cheese
3. Cook pasta and drain it
4. Sit in nettle pesto
5. Transfer onto serving plates and garnish with salt

ONION SOUP

Serves: *4*

Prep Time: *10* Minutes

Cook Time: *30* Minutes

Total Time: *40* Minutes

INGREDIENTS

- 1 tablespoon canola oil
- ½ thyme
- 2 apples
- 5 cups vegetable broth
- 1 onion
- 1 small leek
- ½ tablespoon rosemary

DIRECTIONS

1. In a saucepan heat oil over medium heat
2. Add onions and sauté until golden
3. Pour in the broth and bring to boil over medium heat
4. Add apples and reduce heat
5. Simmer for 10 minutes and remove from heat

ASPARAGUS WITH QUINOA NOODLES

Serves: **2**

Prep Time: **10** Minutes

Cook Time: **30** Minutes

Total Time: **40** Minutes

INGREDIENTS

- 1 bundle asparagus
- 1 tablespoon soy sauce
- ¼ tablespoon sugar
- 3 tablespoons vegetable stock
- 10 oz. quinoa noodles
- 1 tablespoon olive oil
- 2 tsp fresh ginger

- 1 garlic clove

DIRECTIONS

1. In a work heat oil over medium heat and add asparagus and garlic for 2-3 minutes
2. Mix with sugar, soy sauce and stock in a bowl and pour over asparagus
3. Simmer until tender for 4-5 minutes
4. Cook noodles according to package directions and serve

CUCUMER SALAD

Serves: **2**

Prep Time: **10** Minutes

Cook Time: **10** Minutes

Total Time: **20** Minutes

INGREDIENTS

- 1 cucumber
- 1 tablespoon rice wine vinegar
- 1 tsp agave nectar
- 1 tablespoon canola oil
- ½ cup ginger
- chopped leaves
- ½ tsp salt

DIRECTIONS

1. In a bowl mix ginger with cucumber
2. Whisk together canola oil, vinegar, mint leaves, agave nectar and pour over cucumber
3. Arrange in a place and serve

BARLEY SOUP WITH CARROTS

Serves: **4**

Prep Time: **10** Minutes

Cook Time: **30** Minutes

Total Time: **40** Minutes

INGREDIENTS

- 2/3 cup water
- 2/3 cup parsley
- salt
- ½ tsp black pepper
- 2 cups vegetable stock
- 1 cup plain yogurt
- 1/3 cup barley
- 2 tablespoons olive oil
- ½ cup onion
- 1 cup carrots

DIRECTIONS

1. In a saucepan heat olive oil and sauté onion
2. Add spinach, water and bring to boil
3. Cook until spinach is tender

4. Whisk milk and flour in a bowl and pour into saucepan and whisk to blend
5. Bring to boil and simmer, season with salt and pepper
6. Pour soup into bowls and serve

ONION SOUP

Serves: **4**

Prep Time: **10** Minutes

Cook Time: **20** Minutes

Total Time: **30** Minutes

INGREDIENTS

- 1 tablespoon canola oil
- ½ tablespoon thyme
- 2 apples
- 5 cups vegetable broth
- 2 onions
- 1 leek
- ½ tablespoon rosemary

DIRECTIONS

1. In a saucepan heat oil over medium heat
2. Add onion and sauté, add broth and bring to boil
3. Add apples and simmer for 10-12 minutes

CARROT SOUP

Serves: **4**

Prep Time: **10** Minutes

Cook Time: **30** Minutes

Total Time: **40** Minutes

INGREDIENTS

- 2 beets
- 1 tablespoon olive oil
- 1 tablespoon ginger
- 1 garlic clove
- 5 cup vegetable broth
- 1 cup onion
- 1 pound carrots
- 1 garlic clove
- 5 cup vegetable broth

DIRECTIONS

1. In a saucepan heat oil over medium heat, sauté onion until gold
2. Add garlic and ginger and cook for 3-4 minutes

3. Add carrots, stock, beets and reduce heat and cook for 25-30 minutes
4. In a blender add everything and blend until smooth
5. Season with salt and garnish with cilantro and serve

SWEET POTATO SOUP

Serves: **4**

Prep Time: **10** Minutes

Cook Time: **30** Minutes

Total Time: **40** Minutes

INGREDIENTS

- 1 tablespoon canola oil
- 1 large onion
- 1 clove garlic
- 2 tsp curry powder
- 1 pound sweet potatoes
- ½ inch piece ginger
- 2 cups vegetable broth
- parsley

DIRECTIONS

1. In a saucepan heat oil over medium heat, add curry and garlic and cook for 1-2 minutes
2. Add onion, ginger, broth and potatoes and bring to boil over medium heat
3. Reduce heat to low and simmer for 20-25 minutes

4. Puree the soup and serve

BROCCOLI SOUP

Serves: **4**

Prep Time: **10** Minutes

Cook Time: **30** Minutes

Total Time: **40** Minutes

INGREDIENTS

- ¼ cup onion
- 3 cloves garlic
- ¼ tsp marjoram
- 3 cups broccoli florets
- ½ cup barley
- 1 carrot
- 1 rib celery
- 1 tablespoon olive oil
- 4 cups vegetable broth
- 1 can tomatoes
- 1 tsp thyme

- salt

DIRECTIONS

1. In a pot cook onion over medium heat for 2-3 minutes
2. Add vegetable broth and reduce the heat, add carrots, celery and broccoli florets
3. Add barley, garlic, marjoram, tomatoes, thyme and let simmer for 2-3 minutes
4. Remove from heat, season with salt and serve

LENTIL SOUP

Serves: **4**

Prep Time: **10** Minutes

Cook Time: **30** Minutes

Total Time: **40** Minutes

INGREDIENTS

- 2 tablespoons olive oil
- 28 oz. canned tomatoes
- 5 cups vegetable stock
- 1 onion
- 1 carrot
- 2 cloves garlic
- 1 tsp ginger
- 1 tsp cumin
- 1 tsp coriander seeds
- 1 cup red lentils
- 1 tsp salt
- ½ tsp black pepper

DIRECTIONS

1. In a saucepan heat olive oil over medium heat, add onion and cook for 3-4 minutes
2. Add lentils, tomatoes, stock, carrots, ginger, pepper, coriander, salt and bring to boil
3. Simmer for 20-25 minutes and add garlic and cook for another 5 minutes
4. Puree soup in a blender, season with salt and serve

NETTLE & SHALLOT SOUP

Serves: **4**

Prep Time: **10** Minutes

Cook Time: **30** Minutes

Total Time: **40** Minutes

INGREDIENTS

- 6 oz. nettle tips
- 2 tablespoons flour
- 2 shallots
- 2 cups water
- 2 cups milk
- salt
- yoghurt
- 4 oz. spinach
- 2 tablespoons olive oil

DIRECTIONS

1. In a sauce pan heat olive oil, add onion and cook for 2-3 minutes
2. Add water, spinach and bring to boil

3. In a bowl whisk flour and milk and pour into saucepan and whisk to blend
4. Bring to boil and simmer for 4-5 minutes
5. Season with nutmeg or salt and serve

ASPAGARUS WITH QUINCE JAM

Serves: **4**

Prep Time: **10** Minutes

Cook Time: **30** Minutes

Total Time: **40** Minutes

INGREDIENTS

- 2 lb. asparagus spears
- 2 tablespoons fresh ginger
- 2 tablespoon quince jam
- 2 tablespoons olive oil
- 1 tsp lemon juice
- 2 tablespoons walnuts
- salt

DIRECTIONS

1. In a steamer add asparagus and steam until tender for 4-5 minutes
2. In a bowl whisk together, ginger, quince jam, olive oil, salt and lemon juice
3. Pour mixture over asparagus and sprinkle with walnuts

RISOTTO WITH MUSHROOMS

Serves: **2**
Prep Time: **10** Minutes

Cook Time: **30** Minutes

Total Time: **40** Minutes

INGREDIENTS

- 2/4 lb mushrooms
- ¼ parmesan cheese
- salt
- arugula
- ¼ lb zucchini
- 3 tablespoons olive oil
- ¼ cup white wine
- 1 onion
- 1 cup brown rice
- 3 cups chicken broth
- 2 tablespoons parsley
- 1 garlic clover

DIRECTIONS

1. In a saucepan heat olive oil and add zucchini, mushrooms and season with salt
2. Cook for 2-3 minutes and transfer to a plate
3. Add onion, rice and wine and cook for 4-5 minutes
4. Add broth and mushrooms, garlic, zucchini and parsley
5. Transfer to a place and garnish with parmesan and arugula

BROCCOLI SALAD

Serves: **2**

Prep Time: **10** Minutes

Cook Time: **10** Minutes

Total Time: **20** Minutes

INGREDIENTS

- 2 cups broccoli
- 1 cup yoghurt
- 2 tablespoons mustard
- ¼ cup honey
- ½ cup cranberries
- ½ cup sunflower seeds
- 2 apples
- ¼ cup onion

DIRECTIONS

1. In a bowl mix all the ingredients except yoghurt, mustard and honey
2. In a blender add yoghurt, mustard and honey
3. Add dressing to the salad and toss

SMOKED SALMON SALAD

Serves: 2

Prep Time: 10 Minutes

Cook Time: 10 Minutes

Total Time: 20 Minutes

INGREDIENTS

- 1 romaine lettuce
- juice from ½ lemon
- 3 radishes
- 1 carrot
- ½ cucumber
- 1 tsp ginger root
- 1 tablespoon canola oil
- 4 ounces smoked salmon
- 2 tomatoes

DIRECTIONS

1. In a bowl add romaine lettuce, top with radishes, carrots, salmon, tomatoes and cucumber
2. In a jar add canola oil, ginger, lemon juice and mix
3. Pour dressing over salad

CUCUMBER SALAD

Serves: **2**

Prep Time: **10** Minutes

Cook Time: **10** Minutes

Total Time: **20** Minutes

INGREDIENTS

- 2 cucumbers
- 2 tablespoons vinegar
- 1 tsp agave nectar
- 1 tablespoon canola oil
- ½ cup ginger
- mint leaves
- salt

DIRECTIONS

1. In a bowl combine ginger with cucumber
2. Whisk together, agave nectar, vinegar, canola oil and mint leaves
3. Pour over cucumber and ginger
4. Season with salt and marinate for 3-4 hours
5. Remove from refrigerator and serve

SALMON SALAD

Serves: 2
Prep Time: 10 Minutes
Cook Time: 10 Minutes
Total Time: 20 Minutes

INGREDIENTS

- 2 salmon fillets
- 1 cup cucumber
- 1 red onion
- 1 tablespoon capers
- 1 tablespoon dill
- 1 tablespoon balsamic vinegar
- 1 tablespoon olive oil
- ¼ tsp pepper
- salt

DIRECTIONS

1. In a bowl add salmon, cucumber, capers, red onion and toss
2. In a jar add olive oil, vinegar and pour over salmon, toss again

3. Add salt and refrigerate before serving

CARROT FENNEL SALAD

Serves: **2**

Prep Time: **10** Minutes

Cook Time: **10** Minutes

Total Time: **20** Minutes

INGREDIENTS

- 5 carrots
- 1 fennel bulb
- 1 cucumber
- ½ cup mint
- 3 tablespoons lemon juice
- 1 tablespoon canola oil

DIRECTIONS

1. In a bowl mix fennel, cucumber, carrots and mint
2. In a jar add canola oil, lemon juice and pour dressing over salad and toss

CARROT SALAD WITH GINGER

Serves: 2
Prep Time: 10 Minutes
Cook Time: 10 Minutes
Total Time: 20 Minutes

INGREDIENTS

- ½ cup beets
- ½ carrots
- 1 tablespoon apple juice
- 1 tablespoon olive oil
- ½ tsp ginger
- ¼ tsp salt

DIRECTIONS

1. In a bowl mix beets with carrots
2. In a jar mix ginger, olive oil and apple juice
3. Pour dressing over salad and toss

THAI PUMPKIN SOUP

Serves: 2

Prep Time: **10** Minutes

Cook Time: **10** Minutes

Total Time: **20** Minutes

INGREDIENTS

- 2 tablespoons curry paste
- 1 red chili pepper
- 2 15 ounce cans pumpkin puree
- 1 cup coconut milk
- cilantro
- 3 cups vegetable broth

DIRECTIONS

1. In a saucepan cook curry paste over medium heat for 1-2 minutes
2. Add broth and pumpkin and stir
3. Cook for 2-3 minutes and add coconut milk
4. Garnish with red chilies and cilantro leaves

POTATOES WITH POACHED EGGS

Serves: **4**

Prep Time: **10** Minutes

Cook Time: **30** Minutes

Total Time: **40** Minutes

INGREDIENTS

- 2 potatoes
- 15 oz. can tomato sauce
- 4 eggs
- cilantro
- 1-inch ginger
- 1 tablespoon olive oil
- 1 tablespoon curry powder

DIRECTIONS

1. Place the potatoes in a pot and cover with water, boil for 5-6 minutes and drain the potatoes
2. Use a cheese grater to grate ginger
3. In a skillet add ginger, olive oil and garlic, sauté on low heat for 2-3 minutes
4. Add curry powder and sauté for another 2-3 minutes

5. Add tomato sauce and stir to combine, add potatoes and water to the mixture
6. Crack an egg into potato mixture and simmer in the sauce for 10 minutes
7. Remove when ready and top with cilantro

TUNA SALAD

Serves: **4**

Prep Time: **10** Minutes

Cook Time: **30** Minutes

Total Time: **40** Minutes

INGREDIENTS

- 2 5OZ. can tuna
- 1/3 cup mayonnaise
- ¼ cup chopped Kalamata
- 2 tablespoons red onion
- 2 tablespoons red peppers
- 2 tablespoons basil
- 1 tablespoon capers
- 1 tablespoon lemon juice
- salt

DIRECTIONS

1. In a bowl add all the ingredients and stir to combine
2. Serve when ready

TURKEY CHILI

Serves: **4**

Prep Time: **10** Minutes

Cook Time: **30** Minutes

Total Time: **40** Minutes

INGREDIENTS

- 1 tablespoon olive oil
- 1 lb. ground turkey
- 1 onion
- 1 red pepper
- 2 15 oz. cans tomato sauce
- 2 15 oz. cans black beans
- 2 15 oz. cans kidney beans
- 2 15 oz. cans jalapeno peppers
- 2 tablespoons chili powder
- 1 cup corn
- 1 tablespoon cumin
- salt

DIRECTIONS

1. In a skillet heat oil over medium heat and add turkey

2. Add peppers, tomato sauce, tomatoes, onion, corn, beans, chili powder, cumin and jalapenos
3. Stir and season with salt
4. Cook on high heat for 4-5 hours and serve

TILAPIA WITH ROSEMARY TOPPING

Serves: **4**

Prep Time: **10** Minutes

Cook Time: **20** Minutes

Total Time: **30** Minutes

INGREDIENTS

- ½ cup pecans
- 1 tsp olive oil
- 1 egg white
- 4 tilapia fillets
- ½ cup panko breadcrumbs
- 2 tsp fresh rosemary
- ½ tsp coconut sugar
- ¼ tsp salt
- 1 pinch pepper

DIRECTIONS

1. **Preheat oven to 3250 F**
2. **In a baking dish stir in rosemary, breadcrumbs, pecans, coconut sugar, pepper and salt**
3. **Add olive oil and toss to coat the mixture**

4. Bake for 10 minutes
5. In another bowl mix whisk egg white and dip tilapia in the egg white, place the fillets in the baking dish
6. Bake for another 10 minutes, remove and serve

DINNER

ROASTED EGGPLANT DIE

Serves: **4**

Prep Time: **10** Minutes

Cook Time: **45** Minutes

Total Time: **55** Minutes

INGREDIENTS

- 2 eggplants
- 1 tablespoon olive oil
- 5 olives
- 2 cups canned cannellini
- 1 anchovy fillets
- 1 tablespoon lemon juice
- 1 tsp salt
- 1 cloves garlic
- ¼ chopped fresh parsley
- 2 dried tomatoes

DIRECTIONS

1. **Roast the eggplant in oven at 375 F for 40 minutes**

2. In a blender add garlic and eggplant and add olive oil, parsley, tomato, beans, olives and lemon juice
3. Blend mixture until smooth remove and serve

SPINACH SPREAD

Serves: **4**

Prep Time: **10** Minutes

Cook Time: **20** Minutes

Total Time: **30** Minutes

INGREDIENTS

- 2 tsp canola oil
- ½ tsp lemon zest
- ½ tsp pepper
- ¼ grated nutmeg
- ½ cup water
- 2 10-ounce packages frozen spinach
- 1-ounce parmesan cheese
- 1 cup cottage cheese
- 2 tablespoons lemon juice
- 1 cup onion
- 2 cloves garlic

DIRECTIONS

1. **In a skillet heat oil over medium heat and add garlic and onion**

2. Cook for 7-8 minutes an add water and spinach
3. Transfer mixture in a blender and add parmesan cheese, lemon juice, cottage cheese, pepper, lemon zest, nutmeg, salt and puree until smooth
4. Refrigerate at least 4h before serving

LENTIL HUMMUS

Serves: **6**

Prep Time: **10** Minutes

Cook Time: **30** Minutes

Total Time: **40** Minutes

INGREDIENTS

- 1 15-ounce can lentils
- ¼ tsp salt
- ¼ ground cumin
- ¼ cup water
- ½ cup sesame tahini
- 1 clove garlic
- ¼ cup olive oil
- 2 tablespoons lemon juice

DIRECTIONS

1. Mix all the ingredients except water in a blender and blend until smooth
2. Remove and serve

CUMIN SCENTED BEAN DIP

Serves: **4**

Prep Time: **10** Minutes

Cook Time: **10** Minutes

Total Time: **20** Minutes

INGREDIENTS

- 2 tablespoons olive oil
- ½ cup plain yogurt
- ½ tsp cumin
- ¼ tsp garlic
- pepper
- salt
- white beans

DIRECTIONS

1. In a blender add olive oil, white beans, cumin, yogurt, garlic and blend until smooth
2. Season with pepper or salt and serve with cucumber slices or pita

CHIPOTLE BEAN SOUP

Serves: **2**

Prep Time: **10** Minutes

Cook Time: **20** Minutes

Total Time: **30** Minutes

INGREDIENTS

- ½ small onion
- 2 tsp olive oil
- 1 clove garlic
- 2 cups chicken broth
- ¼ chipotle chili powder
- baby carrots

DIRECTIONS

1. In a saucepan sauce onion with olive oil for 2-3 minutes over medium heat
2. Add beans, garlic, chili powder and vegetable broth
3. Add baby carrots and simmer for 12-15 minutes
4. Pure the mixture and season with salt

BEAN AND CORN TACOS

Serves: 2

Prep Time: 10 Minutes

Cook Time: 20 Minutes

Total Time: 30 Minutes

INGREDIENTS

- Beans
- ½ cup corn salsa
- baby spinach
- ½ avocado

DIRECTIONS

1. In a saucepan mix beans with salsa
2. Simmer for 12-15 minutes and serve with tortillas and a pinch of cheese

BLACK BEAN SALAD WITH QUINOA

Serves: 2
Prep Time: 10 Minutes
Cook Time: 20 Minutes
Total Time: 30 Minutes

INGREDIENTS

- ¼ cup dried quino
- 1 cup butternut squash
- 2 tablespoons water
- ¼ crumbled feta cheese
- 2 tablespoons cilantro
- salt

DIRECTIONS

1. In a saucepan add quinoa, squash and water and simmer for 12-15 minutes until squash is cooked
2. Stir in beans and feta cheese and cilantro
3. Remove from heat and season with salt

CREAMY SCRAMBLED EGGS

Serves: 2

Prep Time: 10 Minutes

Cook Time: 30 Minutes

Total Time: 40 Minutes

INGREDIENTS

- 2 tablespoons milk
- salt
- 3 eggs
- 1/3 cup low fat cheese

DIRECTIONS

1. Beat the eggs with milk and salt
2. Cook in a nonstick pan over medium heat
3. Stir in cottage cheese remove and serve

CHICKEN CURRY WITH BROWN RICE

Serves: **2**

Prep Time: **10** Minutes

Cook Time: **20** Minutes

Total Time: **30** Minutes

INGREDIENTS

- 1 cup brown rice
- coconut milk
- 1 tsp curry paste
- vegetable mix

DIRECTIONS

1. In a saucepan simmer sliced vegetables in coconut milk and chicken and add Thai curry paste
2. Remove and serve over brown rice

MEXICAN BROWN RICE

Serves: 2
Prep Time: **10** Minutes
Cook Time: **20** Minutes
Total Time: **30** Minutes

INGREDIENTS

- Brown rice
- Black beans
- 1 avocado
- 1 cup lettuce
- 1 cup shredded cheese

DIRECTIONS

1. Top brown rice with avocado, lettuce, beans and shredded cheese and serve

LEMON ROSEMARY CHICKEN

Serves: **4**

Prep Time: **10** Minutes

Cook Time: **30** Minutes

Total Time: **40** Minutes

INGREDIENTS

- 4 6oz. boneless chicken breast
- 2 tsp olive oil
- 1 tsp lemon pepper seasoning
- 1 tsp salt
- 2 lemons
- fresh rosemary
- 1 cup chicken broth
- ½ tsp garlic

DIRECTIONS

1. Preheat oven to 350 F
2. Brush chicken with olive oil and sprinkle with lemon seasoning
3. In a baking dish place chicken with rosemary and top with lemon slices

4. Bake for 20-25 minutes or until golden brown
5. In a saucepan mix rosemary with chicken broth and garlic
6. Serve mixture with chicken and garnish with lemon slices

PAN CON TOMATE

Serves: **4**

Prep Time: **10** Minutes

Cook Time: **10** Minutes

Total Time: **20** Minutes

INGREDIENTS

- 1 baguette
- 2 beefsteak tomatoes
- 1 clove garlic
- ¼ olive oil

DIRECTIONS

1. Toast the bread and cut the garlic clove
2. Rub with ½ half cut tomato to cover
3. Drizzle with oil and sprinkle with salt

MARINATED CHEESE

Serves: 4
Prep Time: 10 Minutes
Cook Time: 30 Minutes
Total Time: 40 Minutes

INGREDIENTS

- 1 lbs. parmesan cheese
- 2 cups olive oil
- 1 sprig rosemary
- 1 sprig thyme
- 1 tablespoon peppercorns
- 2 dried guindilla peppers or peppers

DIRECTIONS

1. Mix all the ingredients together in a bowl
2. Marinate overnight and store in a refrigerator
3. Serve with toothpicks

MARINATED LAMB SKEWERS

Serves: 2
Prep Time: 10 Minutes
Cook Time: 20 Minutes
Total Time: 30 Minutes

INGREDIENTS

- ½ pound lamb
- 2 cups olive oil
- 1 shallot
- 1 clove garlic
- ½ cup herbs
- 1 pinch saffron
- 1 tablespoon coriander
- 1 tablespoon fennel seed
- 1 tablespoon cumin seed
- 1 tablespoon guindilla pepper
- 3 tablespoons vinegar
- 2 tablespoons lemon juice

DIRECTIONS

1. Skewer the lamb cubes on bamboo skewers
2. Mix all ingredients and pour over skewers and marinade
3. Preheat a grill over medium heat and cook for 2-3 minutes per side

TUNA SANDWICH WITH EGG AND OLIVES

Serves: 2

Prep Time: 10 Minutes

Cook Time: 20 Minutes

Total Time: 30 Minutes

INGREDIENTS

- 1 can tuna
- 1 tablespoon chives
- 1 tablespoon lemon juice
- 1 tablespoon olive oil
- 2 eggs
- 1 tablespoons shallots
- 1 tablespoon capers
- lemon zest
- 2 tablespoons mayonnaise
- salt
- ¼ cup black olives

DIRECTIONS

1. Mix all the ingredients except eggs and guindilla peppers

2. Put the tuna mixture on bread and layer sliced of cooked egg and guidilla peppers
3. Cover with remaining bread and serve

SHRIMP SKEWERS WITH GARLIC

Serves: 2
Prep Time: 10 Minutes
Cook Time: 20 Minutes
Total Time: 30 Minutes

INGREDIENTS

- 2 oz. shrimp
- 2 dried guindilla peppers
- 1 clove garlic
- 1 tsp parsley
- ¼ cup olive oil
- salt
- pepper

DIRECTIONS

1. Skewer shrimp on bamboo skewers

2. Mix the remaining ingredients and pour the mixture over the skewers and marinate
3. Season with salt and pepper and serve

SEEDED RICE

Serves: **6**
Prep Time: **10** Minutes
Cook Time: **20** Minutes
Total Time: **30** Minutes

INGREDIENTS

- 1 cup whole grain rice
- ¼ cup pumpkin seeds
- 2 cup vegetable broth
- ½ tsp salt

DIRECTIONS

1. Rinse rice and drain in colander
2. Place in a bowl and cover with water, soak overnight
3. In a pot mix seeds, rice, water and broth
4. Cook for 45 minutes , remove and serve

SESAME TOFU

Serves: *4*
Prep Time: *10* Minutes
Cook Time: *30* Minutes
Total Time: *40* Minutes

INGREDIENTS

- 1 lbs tofu
- ¼ cup milk
- 2 egg whites
- ½ tsp salt
- ¼ tsp pepper
- 2 tablespoons breadcrumbs
- 1 tablespoon sesame seeds
- 1 tablespoon sesame seeds
- ¼ tsp canola oil
- 12 green onions

DIRECTIONS

1. Cut the tofu into 12 slices and place it in a frying pan, cook over medium heat for 5-6 minutes each side

2. In a bowl whisk together, egg whites, salt, milk, pepper
3. On a plate mix breadcrumbs, black sesame and salt
4. Dip tofu into milk mixture and then into sesame seed mixture
5. Cook for 3-4 minutes
6. Sauté onions for 4-5 minutes and garnish with them

HUEVOS RANCHEROS

Serves: 2
Prep Time: 10 Minutes
Cook Time: 20 Minutes
Total Time: 30 Minutes

INGREDIENTS

- 1 15-ounce can black beans
- ½ tsp cumin
- ¼ cup salsa
- 2 eggs
- 1 corn tortilla
- 2 tablespoons cheese

DIRECTIONS

1. In a pan heat cumin, black means and salsa
2. Cook the eggs and toast with corn tortillas
3. On a plte place the tortillas and top each one with beans egg and cheese

SWISS, HAM AND AVOCADO SCRAMBLE

Serves: **2**

Prep Time: **10** Minutes

Cook Time: **10** Minutes

Total Time: **20** Minutes

INGREDIENTS

- 3 eggs
- 2 tablespoons milk
- salt
- pepper
- 1 slice bacon
- 1 slice Swiss cheese
- ½ avocado

DIRECTIONS

1. In a bowl beat eggs with milk and salt
2. Chop the bacon, avocado and cheese
3. Heat a skillet over medium heat and add egg mixture and cook until eggs are done
4. Add cheese, avocado, ham and cook until cheese melts
5. Remove and serve

DESSERT

RICE PUDDING

Serves: **8**

Prep Time: **10** Minutes

Cook Time: **50** Minutes

Total Time: **60** Minutes

INGREDIENTS

- 1 cup basmati rice
- ½ cup sugar
- ½ tsp cinnamon sugar
- 1 cup water
- ½ tsp salt
- 2 cup rice milk

DIRECTIONS

1. In a saucepan add water, salt, rice and bring to boil
2. Reduce heat and simmer for 45 minutes
3. Add cinnamon, brown sugar and rice milk and cook for another 10 minutes

4. Transfer to a bowl and refrigerate for 2 hours, remove and serve with blueberry sauce

BLUEBERRY SOUP

Serves: 3
Prep Time: 10 Minutes
Cook Time: 20 Minutes
Total Time: 30 Minutes

INGREDIENTS

- 3 cups blueberries
- 2 cup water
- ¼ cup sugar
- 3 tablespoons potato starch

DIRECTIONS

1. In a saucepan add sugar, blueberries, water and bring to boil
2. Mix potato starch with water and stir into blueberry mixture
3. Pour into a serving dish and serve

PINEAPLLE SMOOTHIE

Serves: 2

Prep Time: 10 Minutes

Cook Time: 10 Minutes

Total Time: 20 Minutes

INGREDIENTS

- 2 cups pineapple
- ½ inch ginger
- 1 cup ice
- 1 cup green tea
- 1 tablespoon honey

DIRECTIONS

1. In a blender mix all the ingredients and blend until smooth
2. Remove and serve

APPLE AND RASPBERRY CRUMBLE

Serves: 2
Prep Time: 10 Minutes
Cook Time: 50 Minutes
Total Time: 60 Minutes

INGREDIENTS

- 4 cooking apples
- 1 tablespoon sugar
- 1 tsp cinnamon
- ½ tsp cloves
- 1 cup raspberries
- 1 cup apple juice
- 1 cup oats
- 1 tablespoon butter

DIRECTIONS

1. Preheat oven to 325 F
2. In a baking dish add apple slices and raspberries and pour apple juice over
3. Mix oats and spices in a medium bowl and add butter
4. Add crumble topping over apples and raspberries

5. Bake for 50 minutes, remove and serve

RASPBERRY BANANA SMOOTHIE

Serves: 2

Prep Time: 10 Minutes

Cook Time: 10 Minutes

Total Time: 20 Minutes

INGREDIENTS

- 1 cup raspberries
- 1 cup milk
- 1 tablespoon flaxseed
- 1 banana

DIRECTIONS

1. In a blender add all the ingredients and blend until smooth
2. Pour in a glass and serve

APPLE SLICES WITH CINNAMON

Serves: **2**

Prep Time: **10** Minutes

Cook Time: **10** Minutes

Total Time: **20** Minutes

INGREDIENTS

- 1 apple
- ¼ tsp cinnamon

DIRECTIONS

1. Cut apple into small slices and place them on a plate
2. Sprinkle with cinnamon and serve

QUINOA CREPES

Serves: **4**

Prep Time: **10** Minutes

Cook Time: **30** Minutes

Total Time: **40** Minutes

INGREDIENTS

- 1 cup quinoa flour
- 2 tablespoon canola oil
- 1 tsp baking soda
- 1 tsp cinnamon
- 2 cup water
- 2 cups apple sauce
- cinnamon
- ½ cup tapioca flour

DIRECTIONS

1. Ina bowl mix tapioca flour, baking soda, quinoa flour, cinnamon, water, oil and whisk well
2. In a skillet add oil over medium heat and pour mixture into skillet

3. Cook 1-2 minutes per side remove and serve with apple sauce

BANANA MUFFINS

Serves: 8

Prep Time: 10 Minutes

Cook Time: 40 Minutes

Total Time: 50 Minutes

INGREDIENTS

- 1 cup wheat flour
- 1 banana
- 1/3 cup walnuts
- ¼ tsp salt
- 1/3 cup almond milk
- 1 egg
- ½ cup brown sugar
- ½ tsp baking powder

DIRECTIONS

1. Preheat oven to 325 F

2. In a bowl mix sugar, flour, walnuts, baking powder, salt and mashed banana
3. Add almond milk and egg to mixture and pour mixture into a muffin pan
4. Bake for 35 minutes, remove and serve

ANTIOXIDANT MUFFINS

Serves: *4*

Prep Time: *10* Minutes

Cook Time: *30* Minutes

Total Time: *40* Minutes

INGREDIENTS

- 1 cup wheat flour
- 1 cup blueberries
- ¼ cup almond milk
- 1 egg
- ½ cup sugar
- ½ tsp baking powder
- ½ cup pecans
- ¼ tsp salt

DIRECTIONS

1. Preheat oven to 325 F
2. In a bowl mix salt, flour, powder, baking powder
3. In another bowl beat egg with almond milk and combine with the first mixture
4. Pour batter into paper muffin cups and bake for 30 minutes
5. Remove and serve

CANTALOUPE SMOOTHIE

Serves: 2

Prep Time: *10* Minutes

Cook Time: *10* Minutes

Total Time: *20* Minutes

INGREDIENTS

- 2 cups cantaloupe
- 1 tablespoon honey
- ice
- 1 cup yoghurt

DIRECTIONS

1. **In a blender add all the ingredients and blend until smooth**
2. **Pour in a glass and serve**

CARROT MUFFINS

Serves: **12**

Prep Time: **10** Minutes

Cook Time: **20** Minutes

Total Time: **30** Minutes

INGREDIENTS

- 1 egg
- 1 tsp flaxseed
- 3 tsp baking powder
- ½ tsp salt
- 1 tsp cinnamon
- 1 cup rice milk
- 3 tablespoons canola oil
- 2 cups quinoa flour
- 1 tsp guar gum

DIRECTIONS

1. **Preheat oven to 375 F**
2. **In a bowl beat egg with canola oil and milk**
3. **In another bawl mix the dry ingredients**
4. **Add dry ingredients to dry ingredients and mix**

5. Fill 10-12 paper muffin cups with batter and bake for 20 minutes
6. Remove and serve

TURMERIC SMOOTHIE

Serves: 1
Prep Time: 5 Minutes
Cook Time: 5 Minutes
Total Time: 10 Minutes

INGREDIENTS

- 1 handful of kale
- ½ cup pineapple
- 1 tsp turmeric
- ¼ tsp ginger
- 1 pinch pepper
- 1 spoon chia seeds
- 1 cup almond milk

DIRECTIONS

1. In a blender add all the ingredients and blend until smooth
2. Pour in a glass and serve

PINEAPPLE SMOOTHIE

Serves: *1*
Prep Time: *5* Minutes

Cook Time: *5* Minutes

Total Time: *10* Minutes

INGREDIENTS

- ½ pineapple
- 2 ribs celery
- 1 head romaine lettuce
- 1 handful coriander
- 1-inch ginger

DIRECTIONS

1. In a blender add all the ingredients and blend until smooth
2. Pour in a glass and serve

BLUEBERRY KALE SMOOTHIE

Serves: **1**

Prep Time: **5** Minutes

Cook Time: **5** Minutes

Total Time: **10** Minutes

INGREDIENTS

- 1 banana
- 1 cup kale
- ¾ cup blueberries
- 1 pitted dates
- ½ tsp almond butter
- 1 cup almond milk

DIRECTIONS

1. In a blender add all the ingredients and blend until smooth
2. Pour in a glass and serve

VANILLA PROTEIN SMOOTHIE

Serves: **1**
Prep Time: **5** Minutes
Cook Time: **5** Minutes
Total Time: **10** Minutes

INGREDIENTS

- 1 scoop vanilla protein
- vanilla bean
- 1 cup almond milk
- 1 banana
- 1 tsp green tea powder
- ½ tsp honey

DIRECTIONS

1. **In a blender add all the ingredients and blend until smooth**
2. **Pour in a glass and serve**

BROCCOLI SMOOTHIE

Serves: *1*
Prep Time: *5* Minutes
Cook Time: *5* Minutes
Total Time: *10* Minutes

INGREDIENTS

- 2 ice cubes
- ½ cucumber
- ½ cup apple juice
- 1 handful broccoli
- 1 handful kale
- 1-inch ginger

DIRECTIONS

1. In a blender add all the ingredients and blend until smooth
2. Pour in a glass and serve

TROPICAL SMOOTHIE

Serves: *1*

Prep Time: *5* Minutes

Cook Time: *5* Minutes

Total Time: *10* Minutes

INGREDIENTS

- 1 cup coconut milk
- ½ cup pineapple
- ½ cup mango
- ½ banana

DIRECTIONS

1. In a blender add all the ingredients and blend until smooth
2. Pour in a glass and serve

GREEN SMOOTHIE

Serves: *1*

Prep Time: *5* Minutes

Cook Time: *5* Minutes

Total Time: *10* Minutes

INGREDIENTS

- 1 cup coconut milk
- 1 tsp lime juice
- 1 cup spinach
- 1 cup pineapple

DIRECTIONS

1. **In a blender add all the ingredients and blend until smooth**
2. **Pour in a glass and serve**

BERRY SMOOTHIE

Serves: *1*

Prep Time: *5* Minutes

Cook Time: *5* Minutes

Total Time: *10* Minutes

INGREDIENTS

- 1 cup coconut milk
- 1 cup mixed berries
- ¼ cup Greek yogurt

DIRECTIONS

1. **In a blender add all the ingredients and blend until smooth**
2. **Pour in a glass and serve**

CHERRY PIE SMOOTHIE

Serves: *1*
Prep Time: *5* Minutes
Cook Time: *5* Minutes
Total Time: *10* Minutes

INGREDIENTS

- 1 cup coconut milk
- 1 cup cherries
- ¼ cup oats
- ¼ cup Greek yogurt
- ½ tsp vanilla extract

DIRECTIONS

1. **In a blender add all the ingredients and blend until smooth**
2. **Pour in a glass and serve**

THANK YOU FOR READING THIS BOOK!

Made in the USA
Monee, IL
20 December 2021